YOUR KNOWLEDGE HAS VALUE

Bibliographic information published by the German National Library:

The German National Library lists this publication in the National Bibliography; detailed bibliographic data are available on the Internet at http://dnb.dnb.de .

Imprint:

Copyright © 2016 GRIN Verlag, Open Publishing GmbH
Print and binding: Books on Demand GmbH, Norderstedt Germany
ISBN: 9783656986379

This book at GRIN:

http://www.grin.com/en/e-book/334447/over-policing-among-the-australian-indi-genous-communities

Sa Ngugi

Over-Policing among the Australian Indigenous Communities

GRIN Publishing

GRIN - Your knowledge has value

Since its foundation in 1998, GRIN has specialized in publishing academic texts by students, college teachers and other academics as e-book and printed book. The website www.grin.com is an ideal platform for presenting term papers, final papers, scientific essays, dissertations and specialist books.

Visit us on the internet:

http://www.grin.com/

http://www.facebook.com/grincom

http://www.twitter.com/grin_com

Over-Policing among the Australian Indigenous Communities

Cunneen, (2001) in Australia, the Aboriginal Australians in prisons and courts are grossly over-represented. There have been financial, consultative, and democratic efforts geared towards addressing the issue not only by the Federal Government but also the State. However, despite the efforts to probe on this itching issue for years, no changes have been successfully established. According to Gosford (2011 p1), in the Northern Territory, most youths in custody have been remanded. In a broad view, the problem arises from disrupted work opportunities, cultural and education opportunities, stigmatization, community and family fracture, and social isolation. Thus, Cunneen, (2001), people from the indigenous community continue to die in prison, be incarcerated, sentenced and apprehended in prison. The existing inexorable process is said to have its root cause from the police. While this could be a debatable fact, this research will examine the mode of over-policing among the indigenous people and how that differs from the non-indigenous community in Australia. Thus, the essay supports that the indigenous population is policed differently compared to the non-indigenous people.

From statistics, there is over-representation of the indigenous people within the criminal justice systems in Australia. However, some researches do not concur with the argument and the notion as purported by various individuals. Nevertheless, indigenous over-representation issue has always lagged behind within the public debate and only tragedy incidents or high profile inquiries trigger media coverage of the topic (Alsbury, 2001 p1; Jennett, 1999 p4). For instance, in 1987 the Royal Commission was appointed to investigate such inquiries concerning death rates of indigenous people within police custody. This was so as the death toll among the indigenous detainees in prisons was quite alarming as it amounted to 99 cases. The commission did conclude that, there was over-representation rate among the indigenous people in jail. This led to high mortality rates among the indigenous people in the custody as compared to the non-indigenous communities (Alsbury, 2001 p1). Cunneen (2008 p1), further, the commission found that the police did not offer ultimate care to the detainees while in custody.

Going forward, it is good to understand the general population overview in Australia. According to the 2006 Australian Bureau of Statistics, about 517, 000 Torres Strait Islanders and Aboriginal people did live in Australia. Generally, indigenous people are about 2.5% of the whole Australian population. Inferring from the 2006 indigenous population census, 20, 100 (4%) persons comprised a mixture of Torres Strait Islander and Aboriginal origin, with

33, 300 (6%) being Torres Strait Islander and 463,700 (90%) were of Aboriginal origin. About 32% indigenous people in 2006 resided in main urban centers, with 21% living in inner regional and 22%lived in outer regional localities and 9% and 15% lived in remote and very remote areas respectively. Although, most indigenous people live in urban centers, unlike the non-indigenous population, the indigenous population is highly diverse across the country making up the majority living in the Northern Australia and most areas which are quite remote (Dudgeon, Wright, Paradies et al., 2008 p25).

Unfortunately, indigenous over-representation issue is quite complex with interplay aspects that involve basic causal factors including historical, political, societal and economic factors. Those mostly affected by over-policing behavior live in rural and remote areas (Walker and MacDonald, 1995 p1-3; Albsudry, 2001 p1; Berry and Crowe, 2009 p2). The issue of over-representation remains a burning issue among the indigenous communities. The problem might not be reduced in a night; it requires a long-term approach with active involvement of the criminal justice system participants, police, the government as well as the indigenous people (Nicholas, 2007 p2). Further, the challenge to the solution is that these issues are only tackled when an alarming problem arises and the tasking group only resolves the burning issue and relaxes to await another episode. Thus, the solution to the menace requires fulltime commitment to address the matter regardless of criminal justice issue among the disadvantaged community (Albsudry, 2001 p1).

Studies show that, most of the people behind bars come from very disadvantaged backgrounds. Constituting this category are the Torres Strait Islanders and the Aboriginal Australians. Further, to end over-representation within the system of criminal justice, the issue ought to address the disadvantage peril (Smart Justice, org.au, 2011, p1). According to statistics, the indigenous people compared to the non-indigenous people are 48 times likely to have youth imprisoned, 23.7 times likely to have adult imprisoned, 6.2 times likely to have lower courts incarceration and 9.2 times likely to get arrested (Albsudry, 2001 p2).

Unfortunately, the general indigenous community's population is about 2.5% of the whole Australian population, yet about 90% of those in prisons make up the indigenous community. In the criminal justice system, the young natives are also over-represented. In 1994 June to 1997 June, the number of Indigenous juveniles in detention rose by 20%; with 32% of detained youths in 1999 July being indigenous youths in Australia. Further, the indigenous women are not excluded either in the criminal justice system (Absurdy, 2001 p2). The female gender in the indigenous community is more over-represented compared to their non-indigenous female counterparts as homicide offenders (Mouzos, 2001 p4). This puts a nonsensical picture that indigenous communities are likely to break the law since they are indigenous. Also, this puts forth a contention that there is over-representation of the indigenous people as they are likely to commit a high number of criminal offenses an indicator of oversimplification (Wong. n.d., p3; Absurdy, 2001 p2). Rudin, (2005 p1) this explains the reason why police underestimate the indigenous community and less likely to listen to them. Cunneen, (2005 p134), but what can one make up from a ratio of one police is to 73 persons for instance in Wilcannia in NSW among other remote and rural town? It is over-policing of the highest degree. Hence, over-representation among the indigenous population in the system of the criminal justice can be argued objectively as a result of, "increased rate of recidivism, increased rate of offending from the indigenous people, decreased rate of diversionary program referrals, and in general police and the criminal justice system approach to discriminate against the indigenous community, p2" (Absurdy, 2001 p2).

The Royal Commission of 1991 regarding Aboriginal Custody Deaths identified the historical disadvantage among the indigenous communities in Australia as the primary cause of over-representation (Cunneen 2008 p1). The commission did recommend that to address the difficulties inherent in these traditional communities there was a need for improved housing and health, better education, and increased self-determination. Unfortunately, 20 years down the line Torres Strait Islanders and the Aboriginal Australians not only remain the most disadvantaged communities in Australia but also suffer from exclusion, marginalization, and dispossession experiences. In the years from 2000-2008, there was an increase in the rate of imprisonment by 46% among the women of the Torres Strait Islanders and Aboriginals and 27% increase rate for men in the same population group. In 2008, compared to the non-indigenous population the indigenous community was 13 times likely to be imprisoned. In 2008; 36% youths under supervision in the juvenile justice were from the indigenous community. These statistics are quite disturbing more so because as per survey it was noted that there exist a strong correlation between adult offending and juvenile offending. This is so as one study concluded that in every ten indigenous young people in the juvenile system nine did appear in the adult court in a period of eight years. This rate remains alarming as compared to the non-indigenous the case was nine times more among the indigenous population (Smart Justice.org.au, 2011, p1; Catto and Thomson, 2010 p7).

Over-representation is a present active issue that has yet to face a solution. Questions are all over what causes the problem. According to Smart Justice.org.au, (2011 p1), the over-representation as an issue is caused by a myriad of factors among the indigenous

3

communities. Further, the traditional system of criminal justice has inherent paucity in how it handles the offending. Cunneen, (2006 p332) under the Australian law, indirect racial discrimination, and racial discrimination is prohibited. It would be realistic for the criminologists to investigate this matter and its trade in the unlawful behavior. Indirect discrimination is likely to offer productive research outcome as indirect discrimination prohibition works to combat such acts seen to be "facially neutral" yet have an adverse impact on a group of people or an individual sharing common attributes like race. Various findings show that the indirect discrimination is a reason behind the indigenous population over-representation within the system of the criminal justice. This has been so as is portrayed in the discretionary decision within the system of the juvenile justice as well as the mainstream program provision among the indigenous young detainee programs as the programs provided do not link with the cultural requirement of the youth in the indigenous communities. This could explain the reason behind the Royal Commission inquiry into Aboriginal Deaths in Custody within the 212 recommendation to address the indirect discrimination whose potentiality lays plainly in the existing entrenched institutional practices that have remained unchallengeable for decades. The Equal Opportunity Commission, Human Rights, and the Commission of State Equal Opportunity ought to be motivated to consult this linked Aboriginal legal services and aboriginal organizations with objectives to develop measures that may encourage and facilitate aboriginal people to maximize anti-discrimination models in an effective manner, more so in the aspect of representative action and indirect discrimination.

In regards to indirect racial discrimination, this might be quite enormous arising within the justice, health, training, education and employment. Unfortunately, however, there is little work carried by the criminologists addressing the way forward to indirect racial discrimination within the system of the criminal justice, and that may address the profound unlawful behavior against minorities and indigenous people. Unfortunately as per expertise findings, there is no large crime research firm public-funded as the New South Wales Statistics and Research Bureau, or the Australian Criminology Institute has carried out a survey on the matter. Williams-Mozley (1998 p4), this shows how the government agencies linked with the system of criminal justice have been reluctant to study the issue or remain too sensitive in regards to government-sponsored criminology.

In Simmons, (2009 p1) findings on over-policing did point that those likely to enter in jail among the indigenous community are likely to have been cases of alcohol and drug abuse linking these to indigenous population over-representation in jail among minor issue like

4

street offensive language. The report which raised eyebrows among other keen experts including the Williams-Mozley, a criminologist, and the USQ's indigenous education director pointed loopholes in the report. The reality is that the police are likely to arrest indigenous Australian in a rate 20 times higher compared to the non-indigenous people. From historical perspectives, the policing institution has embraced various practices that result to the indigenous people in Australia leading to their custody and arrest rates over-representation subsequently resulting to the jail population over-representation. Williams-Mozley added that the statistics indicating that about a quarter of men in prisons, a third of women in prison, and 50% of juveniles' detainees are indigenous were truly correct following over-policing. Studies show that the police are highly stationed in various areas in rural and remote centers compared to the urban centers provoking their over-surveillance nature, unlike other areas.

Further, Williams-Mozley pointed the application of discretion as another factor. This arises where racist behavior from individual policemen and women or belief on racism and a focus on a particular legislation by the police as they engage with the traditional indigenous population. Racial discrimination is a reality with police targeting the aboriginal people for public order offending. Substantially, the professor having served in the police for ages does point to a substantial number of prisoners who at the time of offense are intoxicated. However, it is true that about more than a third of the arrested indigenous people are caught while drunk. Allard, (2010 p1) most indigenous persons get drunk during the day unlike the non-indigenous people and thus are highly likely to be caught as police surveillance during the day is enhanced. The outcome of over-representation is known to have come down from many decades of adapting various policy practices and political and societal exclusion. Hence, over-representation among the indigenous community calls upon a national responsibility rather than a particular arm's activity to address the problem (Simmons, 2009 p1).

Among the Australian indigenous communities, policing operates in an environment that understands the residential areas for the indigenous communities not only as cultural entities but, also geographical entities of whom British colonization saw as though they need no protection from the law since the colonial era, (Cuneenn, 2008 p1). As geographical entities, indigenous communities are likely to live in urban centers where there are other cultures or isolated in rural and remote areas with limited facilities and services forcing a challenge to the police (Putt, 2010 p4). This is in line with institutional racism. It's good to understand that with racism it does not refer to a person's attributes or psychological attributes rather points to subordination and domination relationship of exclusion and inclusion. Institutional racism and racism concepts broadly point to social practice. Among the aboriginal community, institutional racism is an institution which embraces habits, practices, and rules that systematically discriminate in one way or the other the already disadvantaged people among the aboriginal community (Cuneenn, 2006 p334; Vivian and Schnierer, 2010 p4).

There has been the wrong focus on an attempt to address over-representation. This is so as overrepresentation among the indigenous communities' policies have on diversion focused on changing the system of the criminal justice system with little emphasis on the reason behind offending behavior. To adequately point out the issue here, Aboriginal over-representation is a multifaceted concept beyond racism or poverty only. In addressing the issue, a person should view the issue from a broad perspective including institutional racism, socio-economic marginalization, structural and historical colonization conditions including single aspect emanating from criminal justice practices and related agencies (Cuneenn, 2006 p334).

The Australian constitution is seen as a key player in contributing to racial discrimination experienced by the Aboriginal people as it purports the ideality of excluding the indigenous community. Indigenous people are seen as a race and to be specific as a mendicant race. This emanates from the Constitution that before 1967 did exclude the aboriginal community from operating via race power (section 51(26) and that from 1967 has been employed as a format of including indigenous community within the constitution. Thus, the Aboriginal identification concerning race and constitution ideas framing in respect to responsibilities, rights, government and citizenship based on races is thus, a contributing issue. This is so as in 1967 while the inclusion of rights was emphasized, the basis of race inclusion was most unfortunate. As thus, race in the clause not only brings a room for misconception but also leads to miss-interpretation to mean something else that could be damaging, on the basis of health, work, and education developing policies geared towards addressing aboriginal marginalization problem. Hence, the author of this collection believes that whether benign or adverse treatment of people as belonging to a specific race should not be part of the foundation for a policy or law. Prior, the race power was a tool for adverse exclusion and discrimination. From 1967 race has been employed as a means for responding to mendicancy and positive discrimination (Campbell, Kelly and Harrison, 2012 p9).

Recapping the disadvantage element, an indigenous Australian has a wide aspect of weakness in all procedures of criminal justice. Referring to earlier studies, it is clear that regarding incarceration rates there are increased rates of Aboriginal people being arrested often compared to the non-aborigines. Further, the aborigines are highly likely to be charged with offenses of 'good order' and in the prisons, they remain over-represented (AIHW: Al-Yaman, Doeland, and Wallis, 2006 p103-106). Policing and aborigines take up a synonym term for years of their use in various aspects. For years, police discretion among the indigenous people is the main factor and cause of the increasing rates of Aborigines apprehension. Looking into the representation of the Torres Strait Islanders and Aboriginal representation within the custody; shows clearly the inappropriate manifestation of the Australian system of criminal justice more so where police powers remain the key determinants of an Aborigine's person within the police custody. This is so as earlier research by Cuneen (2006) shows that aboriginal persons' highest over-representation in police custody remain within the public order offenses area where the discretion of police is the main determinant of whom to arrest or detain and their subsequent charges (Sarre, 2005 p307; Davis, 1999 p5-6).

Police have supreme control and powers over a culture less understood by people from the non-indigenous community, yet the white "seem" to be concerned (Williams-Mozley, 1998 p4). The society class in Australia maneuvers to exercise with oppression models among the indigenous people. The class is fundamental in over-policing issue as it alienates political power among the majority of its traditional citizens and further, applies the system of the criminal justice to coercively maintain an organic order in nature. This is not only a political powerlessness and oppression issue but, ranges from economic to social and racial discrimination among other phenomena (Davis, 1999 p5-6, Allard, 2010 p1).

The strongly rooted problems among the indigenous communities, that is, over-policing and over-representation have seen tremendous funding. For instance, since 2008, the government in Australia together with territories and states has joined efforts to contribute $4.6 billion with an objective of "Closing the Gap". However, despite such tremendous funding, even in subsequent years, the issue remains a problem among the disadvantaged community in Australia. Surveys show that major initiatives among the aboriginal in NSW have shown poor return pertaining the investment level. The conclusion did show that regardless of the recent years' efforts, government coordination is still a challenge. Hence, program service and management delivery remain uncoordinated, with weak linkages between and across agencies.

The separate multitudes of disconnected programs are in contrary to meeting the needs for service delivery flexibility more so in the remote location and form a red tape surfeit. Further, there is exhibited poor communication between agencies regardless of whether their interest and responsibilities are closely related. The outcome frustrates the communities perception of "off the shelf" programs and services imposition and unknown plans on how such services and programs of addressing the disadvantaged communities within the criminal justice system may reach the needy (NSW Ombudsman, 2011 p4).

Generally, indigenous people face violence as victims and as offenders at rates of about 2-5 times compared to the non-indigenous people with higher rates recorded in remote areas. Further, victimization is likely to emanate from various catalyzes like resources accessible to the person, community, and family functionality, individual measures and socio-demographic variables among others. Thus, this factor escalated the violent victimization risk among indigenous people compared to non-indigenous people. Further, the recidivism rate is high among the indigenous people who did undergo imprisonment before compared to the non-indigenous prisoners. About 74% indigenous persons were sentenced before under imprisonment compared to 48% of the non-indigenous people. Incarceration rate remains a concern as the rate among the indigenous people is 15 times more compared to the non-indigenous among the Australians. This is accounted for various factors with some prior pointed out in the essay, but also due to high bail refusal rate, increased remand keeping time, and the system of criminal-justice changes in offending response unlike changes in offending as a factor. Other culminating factors have been within the Australia policing itself. The issue has been that focusing the Australian in general, the system of the criminal justice, police personnel attitude towards indigenous people, various police services hiring, and self-policing (Kiedrowki, 2013, p1). Walker and MacDonald, (1995 p1-3) over-victimization and sentencing biases among the indigenous community as the arrested and those brought before the court are viewed by judges as criminals and lawbreakers lead to the over-representation outcome.

Police diversion in Australia is another aspect. Diversion entails taking an individual through a process that he/she does not face the formal-system of justice reducing the individual's crowding that the system creates. Within the system of juvenile justice, various programs are in place and are applicable at any stage with most of them being employed as pre-court processes. Commonly applied for programs among the young people for processes of diversion entail formal police conferencing and cautioning. Police officers have discretion permission to investigate the type of disposition presented to a juvenile offender. The police are encouraged to employ formal youth justice conferences and police cautions as alternative measures rather than issuing an attend notice or arrest leading appearance in courts. While the police diversion process ought to favor Australians indiscriminately, studies show that there is a disparity between the non-indigenous and young indigenous people who get the opportunity to enjoy the diversion programs. Therefore, there is less likelihood that indigenous juvenile offenders get to enjoy the diversion police process liberty compared to their non-indigenous juvenile offenders. Further, older offenders and males together with offenders with a previous frequency of prior recorded contact hand in hand with those servicing past custodial sentence were unlikely to have their case diverted of which the indigenous people were found to be the majority in this discrimination. The issue is further tied to racial bias within the processes of the criminal justice operation (Stewart, Chrzanowski, Ogilvie, et al., 2009 p3—6).

In conclusion, the indigenous people are policed discriminatively compared to the non-indigenous people. This has not only seen most of them pass through the criminal justice system brutality but also have the majority of them remanded. The burning issue is seen to draw lines from historical aspects deeply-rooted since the colonial era, the socio-economic disadvantage to police mistreatment, and diversion of justice among the indigenous people having a limited chance of justice diversion and the ability to-be-set free. Further, the nomenclature of having more police beeped in remote centers and rural areas with more indigenous groups hold no water. Additionally, the biases within the system of the criminal justice pose more threat to the indigenous people, something that has sidelined the traditional groups as felons and thus as criminals despite the weight of the crime. Frustrations that the indigenous communities face can be accounted for the reasons as to why they are likely to be in the wrong, yet there seem to be fewer policies in place to strategically address the discrimination and the disadvantaged nature that engulf the indigenous communities in Australia, and hopefully the "Closing the Gap" plan will bring a solution to the indigenous disadvantaged situation.

References

AIHW: Al-Yaman, F., Doeland, V. and Wallis, M. 2006. *Family Violence among Aboriginal and Torres Strait Islander Peoples.* Cat. no. IHW17. Canberra: AIHW.

Allard, T. 2010. Understanding and preventing indigenous offending. *Brief,* 9:1-8.

Alsbury, P. 2001. *The Over-Representation of Indigenous People in the Criminal Justice System.* [Online]. http://www.link.asn.au/downloads/papers/indeginous/p_in_01.pdf, accessible 5/30/2016.

Berry, S. and Crowe, T.P. 2009. A review of engagement of indigenous Australians within mental health and substance abuse service. *E-Journal for the Advancement of Mental Health,* 8(1):1-12.

Campbell, P., Kelly, P. and Harrison, L. 2012. No.31 The problem of aboriginal marginalization: education, labour market and social and emotional well-being. Deakin University, Australia.

Catto, M. and Thomson, N. 2010. Review of illicit drug use among indigenous peoples. *Australian Indigenous HealthInfoNet,* 8(4): Article 1

Cunneen, C. 2001. *Conflict, Politics and Crime: Aboriginal Communities and The Police,* Sydney: Allen and Unwin.

Cunneen, C. 2005. *Problems in the Implementation of Community Policing Strategies.* Institute of Criminology; University of Sydney, [Online]. http://www.aic.gov.au/media_library/publications/proceedings/05/cunneen.pdf, accessible 5/30/2016.

Cunneen, C. 2006. *Racism, Discrimination and the Over-Representation of Indigenous People in the Criminal Justice System: Some Conceptual and the Explanatory Issues.* [Online]. http://www.austlii.edu.au/au/journals/CICrimJust/2006/1.pdf, accessible 5/30/2016.

Cunneen, C. 2008. *Policing in Indigenous Communities [2008] UNSWLRS 25.*

Davis, B. 1999. *The Inappropriateness of the Criminal Justice System-Indigenous Australian Criminological Perspective.* [Online] http://www.aic.gov.au/media_library/conferences/outlook99/davis.pdf, accessible 5/30/2016.

Dudgeon, P., Wright, M., Paradies et al., 2008. *The Social, Cultural and Historical Context of Aboriginal and Torres Strait Islander Australians.* [Online]. http://aboriginal.telethonkids.org.au/media/54859/part_1_chapter3.pdf, accessible 5/30/2016.

Gosford, B. 2011. *The 98%-Over-Policing, Suicide and Aboriginal Youth in the NT.* [Online]. http://www.crikey.com.au/2011/11/04/the-98-over-policing-suicide-and-aboriginal-youth-in-the-nt/, accessible 5/30/2016.

Hunt, J. 2013. Engaging with indigenous Australia-exploring the conditions for effective relationships with aboriginal and Torres Strait Islander communities. *Issues Paper No.5 Produced for the Closing the Gap Clearing House.* [Online]. http://www.aihw.gov.au/uploadedFiles/ClosingTheGap/Content/Publications/2013/ctgc-ip5.pdf, accessible 5/30/2016.

Jennet, C. 1999. *Policing and Indigenous Peoples in Australia.* Charles Sturt University, NSW

Kiedrowki, J. 2013. *Trends in Indigenous Policing Models: An International Comparison.* Compliance Strategy Group, Ottawa.

Mouzos, J. 2001, *Indigenous and Non-Indigenous Homicides in Australia: A Comparative Analysis.* Australian Institute Of Criminology Trends and Issues in Crime and Criminal Justice, Australia.

Murray-Ranui, J. 2008. Talking together-relations between police and aboriginal and Torres Strait Islanders in Victoria. A review of the Victoria police Aboriginal Strategic Plan 2003-2008. Office of Police Integrity (OPI) Victoria.

Nicholas, R. 2007. Alcohol and other drug problems among indigenous Australians from rural and remote regions. A policing perspective. Australasian Center for Policing Research.

NSW Ombudsman, 2011. Addressing aboriginal disadvantage: the need to do things differently. A special report to parliament under S31 of the Ombudsman Act 1974. NSW Ombudsman.

Putt, J. (Ed). 2010. Community policing in Australia. *AIC Reports Research and Public Policy Series* 111 p 1-10.

Rudin, J. 2005. *Aboriginal Peoples and the Criminal Justice System.* [Online]. http://www.archives.gov.on.ca/en/e_records/ipperwash/policy_part/research/pdf/Rudin.pdf, accessible 5/30/2016.

Sarre, R. 2005. Police and the Public: some observations on policing and indigenous Australians. *Current Issues in Criminal Justice,* 17(2):305-312.

Smart Justice Org.au, 2011. *Ending Over-Representation of Aboriginal and Torres Strait Islander Peoples in the Criminal Justice System.* [Online]. http://www.smartjustice.org.au/resources/SMART_OverRepresentation_Feb11.pdf, accessible 5/30/2016.

Simmons, A. 2009. *Over-Policing To Blame for Indigenous Prison Rates.* ABC News. [Online]. http://www.abc.net.au/news/2009-06-25/over-policing-to-blame-for-indigenous-prison-rates/1332486, accessible 5/30/2016.

Stewart, A., Chrzanowski, A., Ogilvie, J. et al., 2009. The use and impact of police diversion for reducing indigenous over-representation. *Report to the Criminology Research Council Grant: CRC 15/07-08.*

Vivian, A. and Schnierer, E. 2010. *Factors affecting crime rates in indigenous communities in NSW: a pilot study in Bourke and Lightning ridge.* Community Report, Jumbunna Indigenous House of Learning, Sydney.

Walker, J. and McDonald, D. 1995. *No.47 the Over-Representation of Indigenous People in Custody in Australia.* Australian Institute of Criminology Trends and Issues. Australia.[Online]. http://www.aic.gov.au/media_library/publications/tandi_pdf/tandi047.pdf , accessible 5/30/2016.

Williams-Mozley,J. 1998. *Explanations of Police Racism.* Queensland University of Technology, Australia.

Wong, A. n.d. *The Effects of the Over-Representation of Indigenous People in the Criminal Justice System.* [Online] https://www.uts.edu.au/sites/default/files/com-student-work-wong.pdf, accessible 5/30/2016.